Susan's Growing Up

Sheila Hollins and Valerie Sinason
illustrated by Catherine Brighton

Beyond Words

London

4

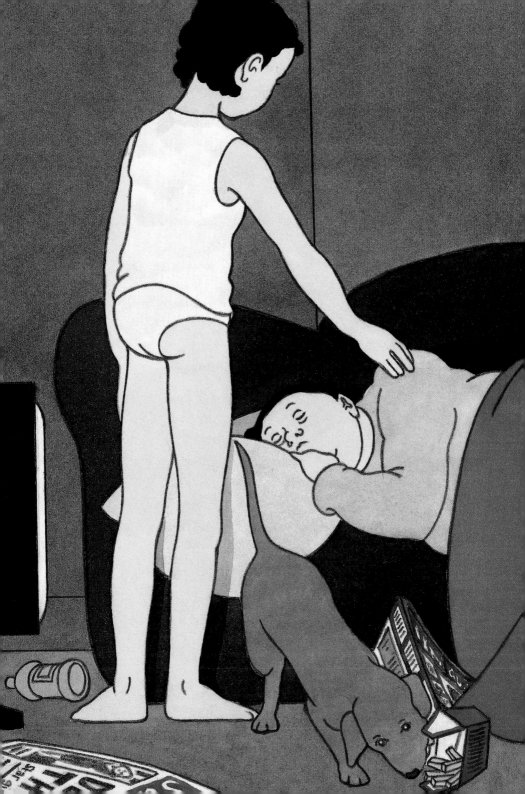

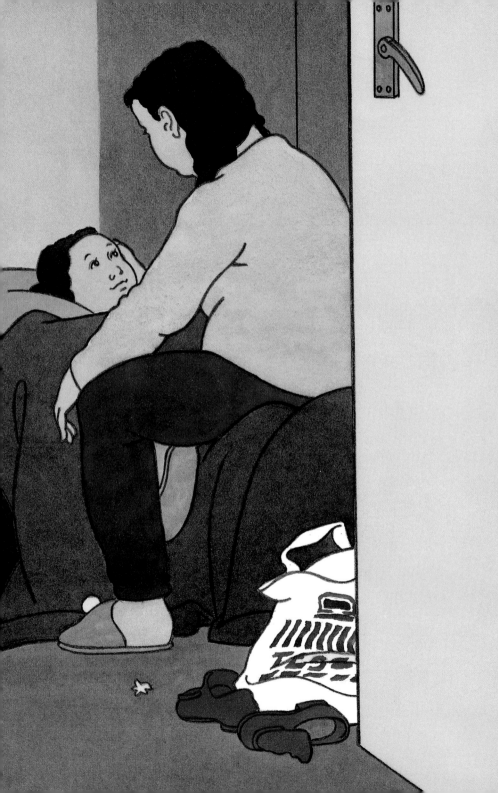

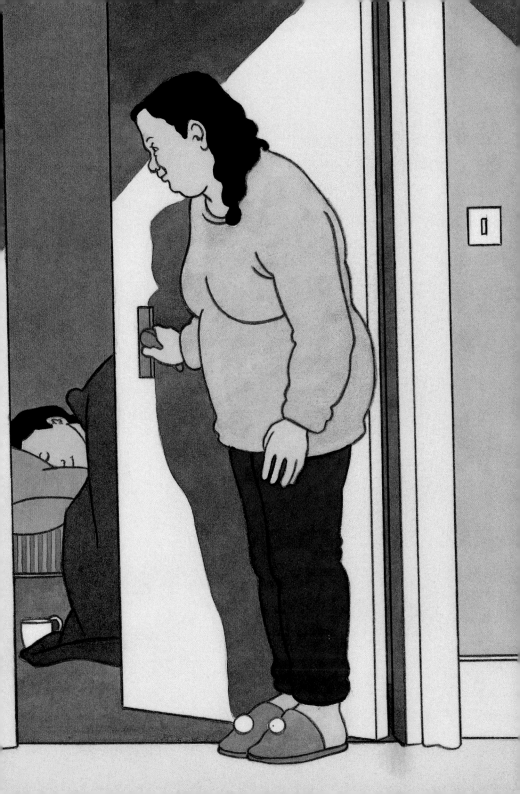

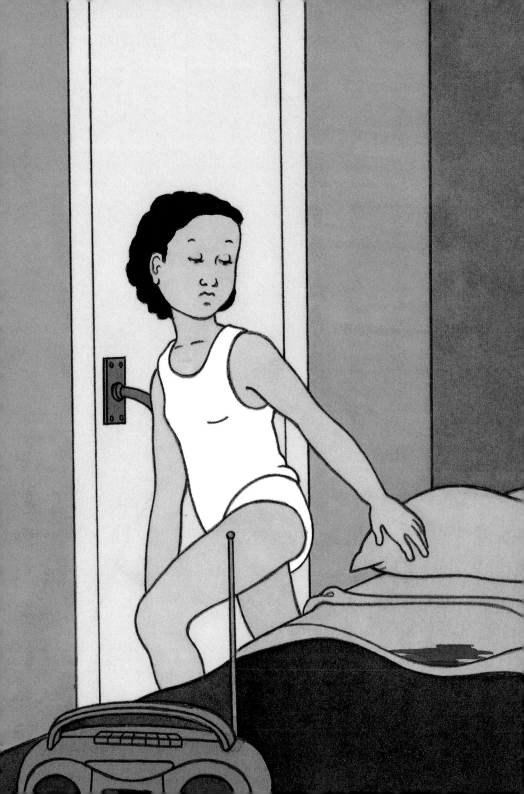

14

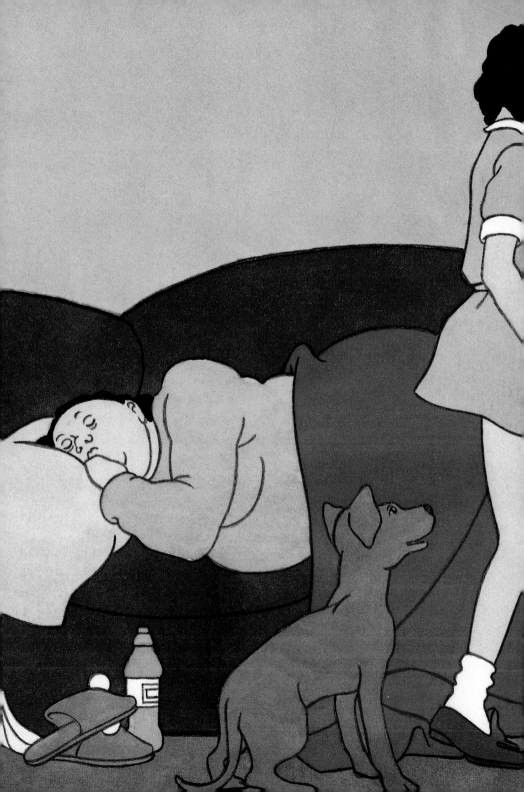

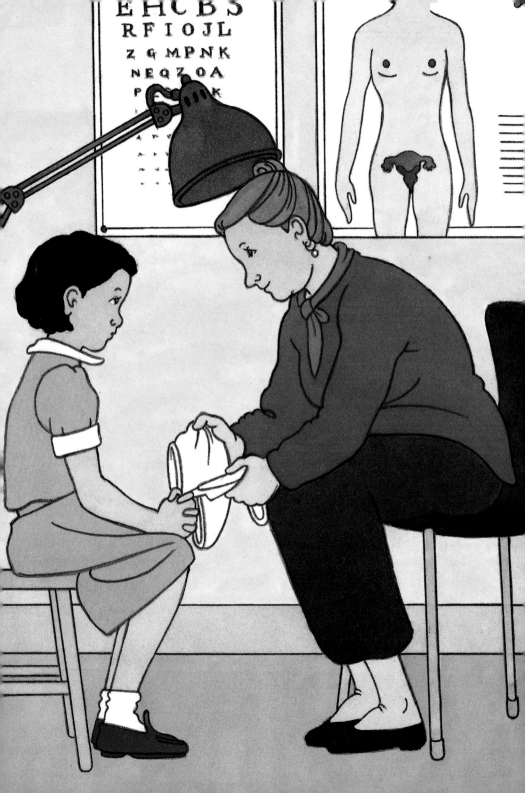

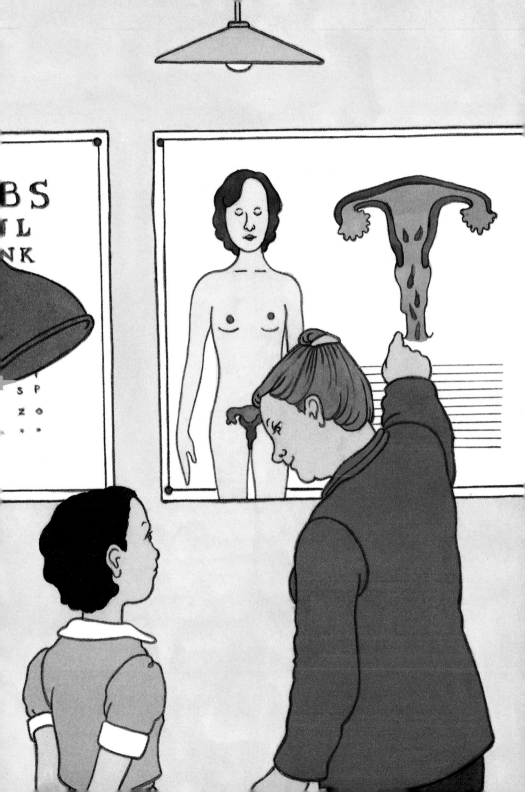

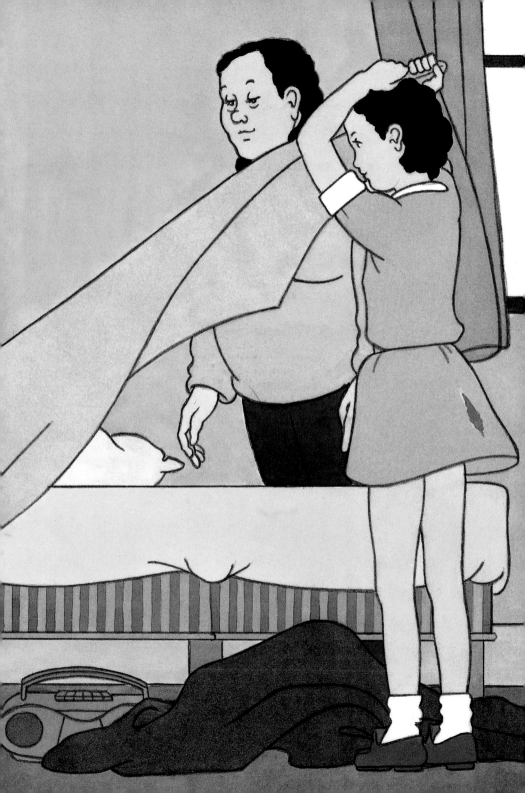

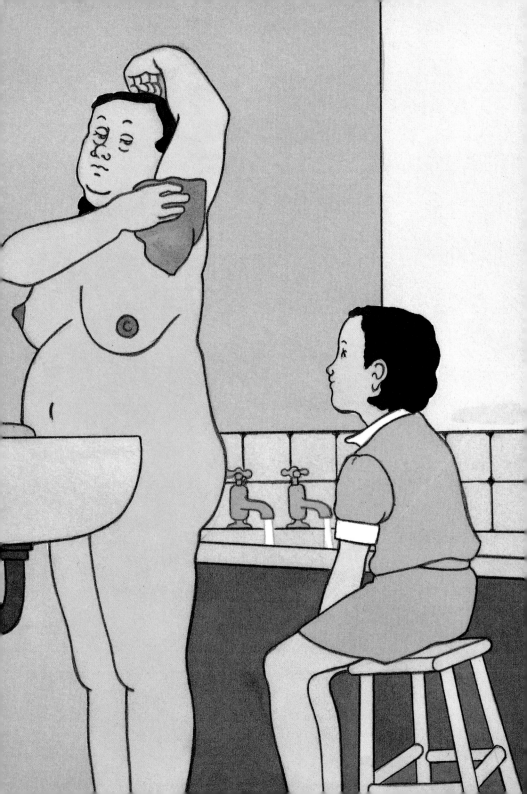

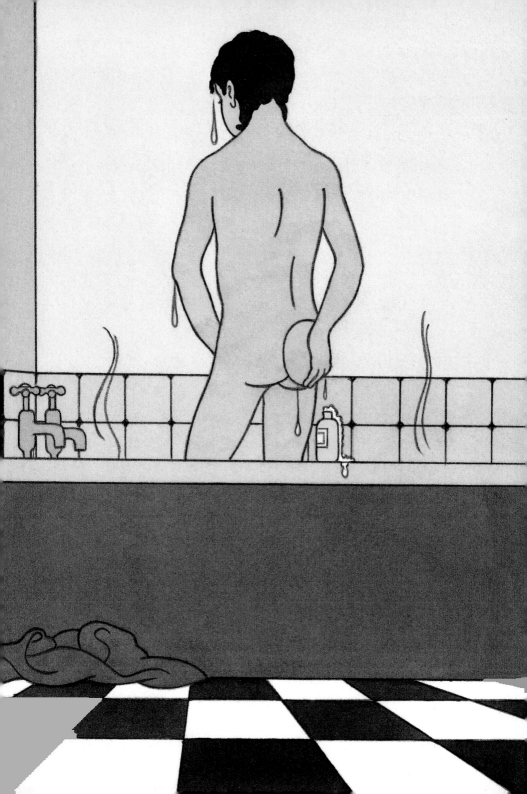

First published in Great Britain 2001 by Gaskell and St George's Hospital Medical School.

This edition published 2019 by Books Beyond Words, charity number 1183942 (England and Wales).

Text & illustrations © Books Beyond Words, 2019.

ISBN 978-1-78458-115-2

British Library Cataloguing-in-Publication Data

A catalogue record for this book is available from the British Library.

Printed by Royal British Legion Industries, Leatherhead.

Gaskell is a registered trademark of The Royal College of Psychiatrists. The Royal College of Psychiatrists (no.228636) is a registered charity.

Further information about the Books Beyond Words series can be obtained from Beyond Words' website: www.booksbeyondwords.co.uk.

Contents   page

Storyline

The following words are provided for readers or supporters who want to get some ideas about one possible storyline.

1. Susan and Mum have a chat and eat their tea.

2. They watch TV together.

3. Susan holds her tummy. Maybe she's got her period.

4. She tells Mum her tummy feels funny.

5. Mum hugs Susan.

6. Susan gets undressed for bed.

7. She sits up in bed. She's got a tummy pain.

8. She wakes up Mum. She needs Mum's help because she feels horrible.

9. Mum's with her – she tries to make Susan feel better.

10. Mum says goodnight to her.

11. Susan looks at her knickers – something's happened.

12. She gets up. There's blood on the sheet. She doesn't know what it is.

13. Susan gets dressed. She's still not sure what's happened.

14. Mum is asleep.

15. Susan has breakfast.

16. She walks the dog.

17. She's off to school.

18. Two friends at school look at some blood on her dress. They talk about her.

19. She goes into the classroom. A teacher stops her.

20. The teacher tells her she's got blood on her dress.

21. She explains that there are stains on Susan's dress because she's got her period. The teacher gives her a pad and clean knickers so that she can change.

22. She shows her a diagram. She explains about periods. She says this is what happens every month.

23. She gives her a book about growing up, and a box of sanitary towels.

24. The teacher phones Mum and tells her that Susan has started her periods.

25. Susan goes home.

26. She's in the bathroom. She changes herself. She gets a pad out of her bag.

27. She wonders how to put it on.

28. Mum comforts Susan.

29. Mum shows her what to do with the pad she has used.

30. They put clean sheets on her bed.

31. Susan watches Mum have a wash. Mum says, "I wash under my armpits".

32. Susan has a lovely bath, with bubbles.

33. She washes her bits and pieces down below.

34. Susan washes the blood off her clothes.

35. She hangs her clean clothes over the bath to dry.

36. They look at the book together. Mum tries to answer her questions.

37. She counts the days until her next period. She looks at the calendar with Mum.

38. They try on bras and tops. It's fun.

39. She's bought her first bra. Hooray. "Now I'm a woman."

Growing up

There are many changes in a child's body as he or she grows from being a child to becoming an adult. This book is to help girls and mothers think about what it is like to become a woman.

Girls and women are different about what changes they like. Most girls grow breasts as they become women. Some enjoy this, and in our book you can see a mother and daughter proud to get new bras. Most girls and women get hair under their arms and between their legs. They notice that they sweat more in these places. It's important to learn how to keep clean and fresh. The most important new thing for most girls is when 'good' blood comes out of their vaginas, showing they are now able to have children physically even if it is several years before they are ready.

Mothers can help their daughters enjoy these new experiences, but if they had bad experiences when they went through these changes themselves they can find it harder to support their daughter through puberty. Reading books like this, helping their daughters to understand what is happening and explaining how to wash and deal with the blood may help many women to grow in confidence and feel happier and more comfortable with their own bodies.

Preparing girls for puberty

It can be hard to know when and how to talk about sexual changes – the ways in which a boy grows into being a man and the ways in which a girl grows into becoming a woman.

Mothers teach their daughters the names of different parts of their body from a young age. It is just as important that they can mention that they are having their 'period' and name their vagina, pubic hair, breasts and other 'private' parts, even if the names they use are personal to them.

As with most things, preparation is key, and teaching girls about what to expect before they start menstruating will make the event much less confusing and alarming when it occurs.

By September 2020, relationships and sex education (RSE) will be compulsory for all schools in England and must be inclusive for children with special educational needs. This book can provide a useful resource to use in the classroom for individual or group learning activities. Several other books in the Books Beyond Words series can be used to support the RSE curriculum (see Related titles).

Useful resources

Services in the UK

Family Planning Association (FPA)
Provides advice and information about women's health problems.
www.fpa.org.uk

NHS information and advice
Visit online or call for help on health issues.
www.nhs.uk
Tel: 111

Materials and online resources

Easy Health
Provides accessible information on a range of health topics, including periods. Three leaflets produced by the Elfrida Society are available to download for free:
- 'Help! I've started my periods'
- 'What is that in my pants?'
- 'What about tampons?'

www.easyhealth.org.uk

'Let's Talk Periods' and 'Let's Talk Puberty' are two free accessible leaflets published by Down's Syndrome Scotland for young people with learning disabilities.
www.dsscotland.org.uk/resources/publications

How to talk to your daughter about her period and puberty. Offers advice and information for parents on how to help girls through the important changes that take place during puberty.
www.tampax.co.uk/en-gb/tampax-articles/parenting-advice

46

Related titles in the Books Beyond Words series

George Gets Smart (reissued 2017) by Sheila Hollins, Margaret Flynn and Philippa Russell, illustrated by Catherine Brighton. George's life changes when he learns how to keep clean and smart. People no longer avoid being with him and he enjoys the company of his work mates and friends.

Going to the Doctor (2018, 2nd edition) by Sheila Hollins, Jane Bernal and Dominic Slowie, illustrated by Beth Webb. This book illustrates a variety of experiences which may occur during a visit to the GP. These include meeting the doctor, having one's ears syringed, a physical examination, a blood test, a blood pressure check and getting a prescription.

I Can Get Through It (2009, 2nd edition) by Sheila Hollins, Christiana Horrocks and Valerie Sinason, illustrated by Lisa Kopper. This book tells the story of a woman whose life is suddenly disturbed by an act of abuse. It shows how with the help of friends and counselling, the memory of the abuse slowly fades.

Jenny Speaks Out (2015, 3rd edition) by Sheila Hollins and Valerie Sinason, illustrated by Beth Webb. Jenny feels unsettled when she moves into a new home in the community. Her supporter and friends sensitively help Jenny to unravel her painful past as a victim of sexual abuse, and begin a slow but positive healing process.

Sonia's Feeling Sad (2011) by Sheila Hollins and Roger Banks, illustrated by Lisa Kopper. Sonia is feeling so sad that she shuts herself off from her family and friends. She agrees to see a counsellor and gradually begins to feel better.

Making Friends and *Hug Me, Touch Me* (both 2015, 2nd edition) by Sheila Hollins and Terry Roth, illustrated by Beth Webb. These books tell the stories of Neil and Janet who want to get to know new people but go about it in the wrong way. The stories tell how they learn when you can and can't touch other people.

Falling in Love (2017, 2nd edition) by Sheila Hollins, Wendy Perez and Adam Abdelnoor, illustrated by Beth Webb. This love story follows the relationship between Mike and Janet from their first date through to deciding to become engaged to be married.

Loving Each Other Safely (2011) by Helen Bailey and Jason Upton, illustrated by Catherine Brighton. Getting close to someone in a relationship is exciting and rewarding. But it's important to stay healthy and safe. This book aims to help young men explore their own sexuality, choose what to do in a steady relationship, and know how to stay healthy.

Finding a Safe Place from Abuse (2014) by Sheila Hollins, Patricia Scotland and Noëlle Blackman, illustrated by Anne-Marie Perks. Katie meets David and falls in love. She moves in with him, but the relationship turns difficult and dangerous when David begins to steal money and hurt her physically. Katie quickly gets help through her GP. After a stay in a refuge, Katie begins a new life with a new sense of confidence.

Authors and artist

Sheila Hollins is Emeritus Professor of Psychiatry of Disability at St George's, University of London, after a distinguished career as a Consultant Psychiatrist in the NHS. She is a past President of the Royal College of Psychiatrists and of the BMA. She is the founder, lead editor and Executive Chair for Books Beyond Words, a family carer and sits in the House of Lords.

Dr Valerie Sinason is a poet, writer, Child Psychotherapist and Adult Psychoanalyst and was Founder Director of the Clinic for Dissociative Studies and President of the Institute for Psychotherapy and Disability. She was given a lifetime achievement award at the International Society for the Study of Trauma and Dissociation. She has published over 150 papers and edited or co-edited more than 18 books.

Catherine Brighton was trained at Central Saint Martins College of Art and the Royal College of Art, and has written and illustrated many children's picture books and other titles in the Books Beyond Words series.

Acknowledgments

We would like to thank our editorial advisers on the first edition of this book, Jackie Downer and Wendy Perez, the Women's Group at Blakes and Link Employment Agency and the 'You're in Charge' group at Speedwell RAC in Bristol for helping us think of ideas and for telling us what was needed in the pictures.

For giving her time so generously, our grateful thanks remain with Jackie Rodgers from the Norah Fry Research Centre, Bristol.

Finally, the original development of *Susan's Growing Up* would not have been possible without a generous grant from the Department of Health.

Beyond Words: publications and training

Books Beyond Words are stories for anyone who finds pictures easier than words. A list of all Beyond Words publications, including print and eBook versions of Books Beyond Words titles, and where to buy them, can be found on our website:

www.booksbeyondwords.co.uk

Workshops co-taught by trainers with learning disabilities for family carers, support workers and professionals can be provided on request. Self-advocates are always welcome. E-learning modules about using Books Beyond Words will also be useful for some people. For information about training and e-learning, please contact us:

email: admin@booksbeyondwords.co.uk

Video clips showing our books being read are also on our website and YouTube channel: www.youtube.com/user/booksbeyondwords.

How to read this book

This is a story for people who find pictures easier to understand than words. It is not necessary to be able to read any words at all.

1. Some people are not used to reading books. Start at the beginning and read the story in each picture. Encourage the reader to hold the book themselves and to turn the pages at their own pace.

2. Whether you are reading the book with one person or with a group, encourage them to tell the story in their own words. You will discover what each person thinks is happening, what they already know, and how they feel. You may think something different is happening in the pictures yourself, but that doesn't matter. Wait to see if their ideas change as the story develops. Don't challenge the reader(s) or suggest their ideas are wrong.

3. Some pictures may be more difficult to understand. It can help to prompt the people you are supporting, for example:

- I wonder who that is?
- I wonder what is happening?
- What is he or she doing now?
- I wonder how he or she is feeling?
- Do you feel like that? Has it happened to you/ your friend/ your family?

4. You don't have to read the whole book in one sitting. Allow people enough time to follow the pictures at their own pace.

5. Some people will not be able to follow the story, but they may be able to understand some of the pictures. Stay a little longer with the pictures that interest them.